EXPLORE

KEFALONIA

Travel Guide

The Citi-scaper

The Citi-scaper Travel Guide

Copyright © 2023 by The Citi-scaper

Disclaimer

The information contained in this travel guide is for general information purposes only. It is not intended to be a substitute for professional advice or medical treatment.

The author and publisher of this travel guide make no representations or warranties regarding the accuracy, completeness, or suitability of the information contained herein. The information is provided on an "as is" basis, and the author and publisher disclaim all liability for any loss or damage that may result from the use of this information.

The travel guide may contain links to other websites. The author and publisher of this travel guide have no control over the content of these websites and disclaim any liability for any loss or damage that may result from the use of these websites.

The author and publisher of this travel guide reserve the right to make changes to the information contained herein at any time without notice.

Table of Contents

INTRODUCTION

Welcome to the enchanting island of Kefalonia!

Nestled in the turquoise waters of the Ionian Sea, this Greek paradise beckons travelers seeking natural beauty, rich history, and warm Mediterranean hospitality. This travel guidebook is your key to unlocking the secrets of Kefalonia, offering a carefully curated collection of information, tips, and insider knowledge to ensure an unforgettable journey.

Whether you're an adventure enthusiast looking to hike the island's dramatic cliffs or a culture connoisseur eager to delve into Kefalonia's artistic and literary heritage, this guidebook has you covered. From the breathtaking Melissani Cave to the impressive Assos Castle, each attraction is described in detail, allowing you to plan your itinerary with ease. Discover hidden gems off the beaten path, from secret coves to tranquil monasteries, ensuring you experience Kefalonia beyond its well-known landmarks.

To make your trip seamless, practical information on transportation, accommodations, dining options, and local customs are also included. This guidebook provides valuable insights tailored to your travel preferences.

Prepare to be captivated by Kefalonia's natural wonders, embraced by its warm-hearted locals, and immersed in its rich cultural tapestry. Let this travel guidebook be your trusted companion as you embark on an extraordinary journey through the magical island of Kefalonia.

CHAPTER 1

OVERVIEW OF KEFALONIA

History and Culture

Steeped in a captivating tapestry of history and culture, Kefalonia offers a remarkable journey through the ages. From ancient civilizations to Byzantine influences and modern Greek traditions, the island's past has shaped its unique identity.

Kefalonia's rich history dates back to the Mycenaean period, with archaeological sites revealing glimpses of the island's ancient past. Explore the remains of ancient settlements such as Sami and Krani, where you can trace the footsteps of civilizations that once thrived on this land.

During the Byzantine era, Kefalonia became an important center of religious activity, leaving behind numerous monasteries and churches adorned with intricate frescoes and icons. Marvel at the spiritual beauty of the Monastery of Agios Gerasimos, dedicated to the patron saint of the island, or visit the Monastery of Panagia Agrilion, perched on a hilltop offering breathtaking vistas.

In more recent history, Kefalonia experienced the impact of various civilizations and foreign occupations. The island played a role in the Venetian Republic and later became part of the Ottoman Empire. Explore the charming Venetian-inspired architecture in the town of Argostoli, or visit the Kastro of St. George, a medieval fortress offering panoramic views.

Kefalonia also bears the scars of World War II and the devastating earthquakes of 1953. The island's resilient spirit is evident in the reconstructed villages and the stoic resilience of its people, who have preserved their traditions and cultural heritage.

Allow yourself to be immersed in Kefalonia's history and culture, where each step reveals layers of the island's intriguing past. From ancient ruins to living traditions, this enchanting destination invites you to embark on an enriching journey through time.

Geography and Climate

Nestled in the heart of the Ionian Sea, Kefalonia boasts a breathtaking natural landscape that captivates visitors from around the world. The island's geography showcases a diverse tapestry of stunning vistas, dramatic coastlines, and picturesque mountains.

Covering an area of approximately 781 square kilometers, Kefalonia is the largest of the Ionian Islands and offers a varied terrain to explore. The island is defined by its mountainous backbone, with the majestic Mount Ainos standing as its highest peak, reaching an elevation of 1,628 meters. Embark on exhilarating hikes through lush forests, where rare flora and fauna thrive, or take in panoramic views from scenic lookout points.

Kefalonia's coastline is a treasure trove of natural beauty, with pristine beaches that beckon sun-seekers and water enthusiasts. From the famous Myrtos Beach, with its striking cliffs and azure waters, to secluded coves like Assos and Foki, each beach offers its own charm and allure.

The island's climate is classified as Mediterranean, blessed with mild winters and long, hot summers. From May to September, the sun-drenched days and pleasant temperatures create the perfect environment for beachside relaxation and outdoor activities. During the summer months, temperatures can soar, reaching highs of around 30°C (86°F), making it an ideal time for swimming, snorkeling, and exploring the island's natural wonders.

Autumn and spring bring milder temperatures and occasional rainfall, painting the landscape with lush greenery and blooming wildflowers. These seasons are ideal for hiking and exploring the island's diverse flora and fauna. Winter, although quieter in terms of tourism, reveals a different side of Kefalonia, with cooler temperatures and the opportunity to experience the island's authentic local life.

Kefalonia's unique geography and favorable climate create an inviting backdrop for outdoor adventures, from leisurely walks along coastal trails to challenging mountain hikes. Immerse yourself in the island's natural wonders, as you discover the hidden gems and breathtaking panoramas that make Kefalonia a true paradise for nature enthusiasts.

Embrace the diverse geography and delightful climate of Kefalonia as you embark on unforgettable explorations across its stunning landscapes. From mountain peaks to turquoise shores, this captivating island offers a world of natural beauty waiting to be discovered.

When to Visit

Kefalonia welcomes visitors throughout the year, each season offering its own unique experiences and attractions. The best time to visit depends on your preferences and the type of activities you wish to pursue.

Summer, from June to August, is the peak tourist season in Kefalonia. During these months, the island basks in warm temperatures, ranging from 25°C to 30°C (77°F to 86°F), and the sea is perfect for swimming and water sports. The beaches come alive, and the vibrant atmosphere fills the coastal towns and villages. However, it's important to note that this period can be quite busy, with larger crowds and higher accommodation prices.

For those seeking a balance between pleasant weather and fewer tourists, the shoulder seasons of spring (April to May) and autumn (September to October) are excellent times to visit. During these months, temperatures range from 18°C to 25°C (64°F to 77°F), creating comfortable conditions for exploring the island's attractions, hiking, and enjoying outdoor activities.

Winter, from November to March, is considered the low season in Kefalonia. While the temperatures are cooler, ranging from 10°C to 16°C (50°F to 61°F), the island offers a tranquil ambiance ideal for those seeking a peaceful retreat. Winter is a great time to immerse yourself in the local culture, experience authentic traditions, and enjoy the island's natural beauty without the crowds. Keep in mind that some tourist facilities and services may have reduced availability during this time.

Ultimately, the best time to visit Kefalonia depends on your personal preferences. Consider the activities you wish to engage in, your desired level of crowd and budget, and the overall experience you seek, and plan your visit accordingly.

Petani Beach

CHAPTER 2

ESSENTIAL PREPARATIONS

Planning Your Trip

Planning your trip to Kefalonia is an exciting step towards an unforgettable adventure. To ensure a smooth and enjoyable experience, here are some essential preparations to consider:

Research and gather information: Start by researching Kefalonia's attractions, activities, and points of interest.

Look into the island's history, culture, and local customs to better understand its unique character. Familiarize yourself with transportation options, accommodation choices, and dining recommendations. Utilize travel websites, guidebooks, and online forums to gather valuable insights and recommendations from fellow travelers.

Determine the duration of your stay: Consider how much time you have available for your trip. Kefalonia offers a variety of experiences, and the duration of your stay will influence the activities and destinations you can explore. Factor in travel time, allowing yourself ample opportunity to immerse in the island's beauty without feeling rushed.

Choose the best time to visit: Consider the weather, your preferred level of tourist activity, and the type of experience you desire when deciding on the best time to visit Kefalonia. Evaluate the pros and cons of each season, whether you prefer the bustling summer months, the mild shoulder seasons, or the peaceful ambiance of winter. Select a time that aligns with your preferences and expectations.

Create an itinerary: Outline a rough itinerary to help you make the most of your time on the island. Identify the attractions, beaches, and landmarks you wish to visit, and allocate sufficient time for each. Be mindful of travel distances and factor in relaxation time as well. Remember to leave room for spontaneous exploration and relaxation, as unexpected discoveries often enhance the travel experience.

Arrange transportation: Explore transportation options to reach Kefalonia and move around the island. The island is served by Kefalonia International Airport, which offers domestic and international flights. Additionally, ferry services connect Kefalonia to other Greek islands and mainland ports. Depending on your preferences, you can rent a car, use public transportation, or hire taxis to navigate the island. Research and book your preferred mode of transportation in advance to ensure availability.

Book accommodations: Research and book accommodations that suit your preferences and budget. Kefalonia offers a range of options, from luxury resorts and boutique hotels to budget-friendly guesthouses and self-catering apartments. Consider factors such as location, amenities, and reviews to find the perfect place to stay. Booking in advance is recommended, especially during peak tourist seasons.

Check travel requirements and documents: Ensure that you have all the necessary travel documents in order. Check visa requirements, passport validity, and any specific entry requirements for Greece. It's also advisable to have travel insurance to protect yourself against unforeseen circumstances.

By following these essential preparations and planning your trip to Kefalonia thoughtfully, you'll be well-equipped to make the most of your time on the island.

Packing Tips

When preparing for your trip to Kefalonia, here are some packing tips and essential items to consider bringing:

Clothing: Pack lightweight and breathable clothing suitable for the Mediterranean climate. Include comfortable walking shoes for exploring the island's attractions and beaches. Don't forget swimwear, a hat, sunglasses, and a beach towel for enjoying the sun and sea. Additionally, consider bringing a light jacket or sweater for cooler evenings or unexpected weather changes.

Travel essentials: Bring your passport, visa (if required), and travel insurance documents. Carry a copy of your itinerary, accommodation reservations, and important contact information. Remember to pack any necessary medications, along with a small first aid kit containing band-aids, pain relievers, and any specific medications you may need.

Electronics: Don't forget to bring your camera or smartphone to capture the stunning landscapes of Kefalonia. Remember to pack the necessary charging cables and adapters for your devices. A portable power bank can also be useful for staying connected while on the go.

Beach essentials: Kefalonia boasts beautiful beaches, so pack beach essentials such as sunscreen (preferably reef-safe), a beach bag, a beach umbrella or sunshade, and a reusable water bottle to stay hydrated.

Other useful items: Bring a reusable shopping bag for groceries or souvenirs. A travel guidebook or map can be helpful for navigating the island. Consider packing insect repellent, especially if you plan to spend time outdoors or in rural areas.

Travel Documents and Visas

When planning your trip to Kefalonia, it's important to ensure you have the necessary travel documents and visas in order to enter Greece. Here are some essential details to consider:

Passport: Ensure that your passport is valid for at least six months beyond your intended departure date from Greece. It's important to check your passport's validity well in advance and renew it if needed.

Visa requirements: Greece is part of the Schengen Area, which allows travelers from many countries to enter without a visa for short stays of up to 90 days within a 180-day period. However, visa requirements vary depending on your nationality. Check the official website of the Greek Ministry of Foreign Affairs or consult the nearest

Greek embassy or consulate in your country to determine if you need a visa for your visit to Kefalonia.

Visa application: If you require a visa, start the application process well ahead of your planned travel dates. Contact the Greek embassy or consulate in your country for specific instructions and requirements. Prepare all necessary documentation, including completed application forms, passport photos, proof of accommodation, travel itinerary, proof of financial means, and travel insurance. Submit your application within the designated time frame to allow for processing.

Keep copies of important documents: Make copies of your passport, visa, travel insurance, and other important documents. Store these copies separately from the originals and also consider keeping digital copies in your email or cloud storage for easy access.

It's crucial to verify all the visa and travel document requirements well in advance of your trip to Kefalonia. Being well-prepared will help you have a smooth and hassle-free journey to this beautiful Greek island.

Health and Safety Considerations

To ensure your health and safety during your visit to Kefalonia, keep the following considerations in mind:

Medical care: Familiarize yourself with the location of medical facilities, clinics, and pharmacies on the island. Carry a copy of your travel insurance information and any necessary medical prescriptions or documentation.

Drinking water: Tap water in Kefalonia is generally safe to drink, but if you prefer, you can opt for bottled water, which is widely available.

Sun protection: The Mediterranean sun can be intense, so protect yourself by applying sunscreen with a high SPF, wearing a hat, and seeking shade during the hottest hours of the day.

Emergency contacts: Keep a list of emergency contacts, including local authorities, your embassy or consulate, and your accommodation's contact information.

Currency and Money Matters

The currency of Greece is the Euro (€). Here are some currency and money-related tips for your trip to Kefalonia:

Currency exchange: It's advisable to exchange your currency to Euros before arriving in Kefalonia. You can do this at your local bank or currency exchange office. Alternatively, you'll find ATMs (automated teller machines) in major towns and tourist areas where you can withdraw Euros using your debit or credit card.

Credit cards: Credit cards are widely accepted in hotels, restaurants, and larger establishments in Kefalonia. However, it's always good to carry some cash, especially for smaller shops, markets, and local establishments that may prefer cash payments.

ATMs: ATMs are commonly found throughout Kefalonia, allowing you to withdraw Euros as needed. Be mindful of any withdrawal fees or foreign transaction charges imposed by your bank.

Budgeting: Determine your daily budget based on your planned activities, meals, and accommodations. Take into account the cost of dining out, transportation, and any entrance fees for attractions you wish to visit.

Tipping: Tipping is customary in Greece, but it's not obligatory. If you receive good service, it's common to leave a small tip of around 5-10% of the total bill. However, it's always discretionary and based on your satisfaction.

By considering these packing tips, health and safety considerations, and currency matters, you'll be well-prepared for your trip to Kefalonia. Remember to prioritize your well-being, stay informed about local guidelines and regulations, and make the most of your time on this beautiful Greek island.

CHAPTER 3

EXPLORING KEFALONIA'S REGIONS

Argostoli

Argostoli, the capital and main port of Kefalonia, is a vibrant and bustling town that offers a blend of history, culture, and natural beauty. Its population is over 10,000. Here are some highlights to explore in Argostoli:

Lithostroto: Begin your exploration on Lithostroto, the main pedestrian street of Argostoli. This lively avenue is lined with shops, cafes, and restaurants, perfect for strolling and enjoying the local ambiance.

Koutavos Lagoon: Head to the waterfront promenade to discover the beautiful Koutavos Lagoon. This serene natural reserve is home to a variety of bird species, and you can admire them from the wooden bridge or take a boat tour to get closer to the wildlife.

Drapano Bridge: Don't miss the iconic De Bosset Bridge, also known as the Drapano Bridge, which connects Argostoli with the opposite side of the lagoon. This historical stone bridge is a popular spot for walks and offers splendid views of the lagoon and the town.

Drapano Bridge

Archaeological Museum: Visit the Archaeological Museum of Argostoli to delve into the island's ancient history. Discover artifacts from excavations around Kefalonia, including pottery, sculptures, and tomb relics that shed light on the island's past civilizations.

Stroll along the Harborfront: Take a leisurely stroll along the harborfront, lined with charming cafes and seafood restaurants. Enjoy the picturesque views of the fishing boats and yachts, and watch the sunset paint the sky with breathtaking colors.

Lixouri

Located on the Paliki Peninsula, Lixouri is a charming town known for its laid-back atmosphere, stunning beaches, and traditional Greek hospitality. It is the second largest city in Kefalonia. Here are some attractions to explore in Lixouri:

Lixouri Town Square: Begin your journey in Lixouri at the bustling town square, Plateia Petritsi. Admire the neoclassical architecture, relax in the shade of the plane trees, and enjoy a coffee or a refreshing drink at one of the local cafes.

Ethnikis Antistaseos Street: Explore the main street of Lixouri, Ethnikis Antistaseos, lined with shops, boutiques, and traditional tavernas. Discover local products, souvenirs, and indulge in delicious Kefalonian cuisine.

Lepeda Beach: Just a short distance from Lixouri, you'll find Lepeda Beach, a picturesque sandy shore with crystal-clear waters. Spend a relaxing day sunbathing, swimming, or enjoying water sports in this idyllic coastal spot.

Xi Beach: Xi Beach is another popular beach near Lixouri, known for its unique reddish-orange sand and shallow waters. The beach is well-equipped with sunbeds, umbrellas, and beach bars, making it an ideal spot for a day of relaxation and seaside enjoyment.

Monastery of Kipoureon: Venture slightly outside Lixouri to visit the Monastery of Kipoureon, perched on a cliff with panoramic views of the Ionian Sea. This 17th-century monastery is a place of tranquility and offers a glimpse into the island's religious heritage.

Exploring Argostoli and Lixouri allows you to experience different facets of Kefalonia's charm. Whether it's strolling through the vibrant streets of the capital or enjoying the laid-back coastal vibe of Lixouri, these regions offer a delightful blend of history, natural beauty, and local culture.

Sami

Sami, located on the eastern coast of Kefalonia, is a picturesque town known for its natural beauty, historical sites, and tranquil atmosphere. Here are some attractions to explore in Sami:

Melissani Cave: One of the most iconic attractions in Kefalonia, the Melissani Cave is a stunning underground lake with crystal-clear turquoise waters. Take a boat tour through the cave's enchanting chambers and marvel at the mesmerizing play of light and shadows.

Melissani Cave

Antisamos Beach: Just a short distance from Sami, you'll find Antisamos Beach, a breathtaking stretch of pebbly shoreline framed by lush hills. The azure waters and beautiful surroundings make it a popular spot for swimming, sunbathing, and water sports.

Ancient Sami: Immerse yourself in history by exploring the archaeological site of Ancient Sami, located just outside the town. Discover the remains of ancient walls, Roman baths, and other structures that offer insights into the island's past civilizations.

Drogarati Cave: Visit the Drogarati Cave, an impressive natural wonder near Sami. Admire the stalactites and stalagmites as you explore the illuminated chambers, and be amazed by the exceptional acoustics that have made the cave a popular concert venue.

Explore the Town: Take a leisurely stroll through the charming streets of Sami, lined with colorful houses, quaint cafes, and inviting tavernas. Enjoy a meal of freshly caught seafood or sample local delicacies in the town's traditional eateries.

Fiscardo

Fiscardo is one of the over 300 villages in Kefalonia. It is located on the northern tip of Kefalonia, is a picturesque fishing village renowned for its Venetian architecture, scenic harbor, and cosmopolitan atmosphere. Here are some attractions to explore in Fiscardo:

Fiscardo Harbor: Start your exploration by taking in the idyllic views of Fiscardo Harbor, adorned with colorful fishing boats and luxurious yachts. Relax at one of the waterfront cafes or tavernas, savoring the delightful ambiance of this charming village.

Venetian Lighthouse: Walk to the Venetian Lighthouse, perched on a rocky outcrop overlooking the harbor. Enjoy panoramic views of the Ionian Sea and capture memorable photos of the coastline and surrounding landscapes.

Traditional Architecture: Wander through Fiscardo's narrow streets and admire the beautifully preserved Venetian architecture. The vibrant facades, quaint balconies, and red-tiled roofs create a picturesque setting that exudes old-world charm.

Assos Castle: Take a short drive south of Fiscardo to visit the impressive Assos Castle. This 16th-century fortress sits atop a hill, offering panoramic views of the surrounding area. Explore the ruins and imagine the castle's historic significance.

Emblisi Beach: Relax and soak up the sun at Emblisi Beach, located within walking distance of Fiscardo. This secluded beach features turquoise waters and is surrounded by verdant hills, providing a tranquil escape.

Exploring the regions of Sami and Fiscardo allows you to uncover the diverse beauty and history of Kefalonia. From natural wonders like Melissani Cave and Antisamos Beach to the charming streets of Fiscardo, each destination offers a unique experience that adds to the allure of this enchanting island.

Assos

Nestled on a scenic peninsula on the western coast of Kefalonia, Assos is a charming village known for its idyllic setting, Venetian architecture, and historical landmarks. Here are some attractions to explore in Assos:

Assos Castle: The highlight of Assos is the impressive Assos Castle, perched on a hilltop overlooking the village and the sea. Dating back to the 16th century, this Venetian fortress offers panoramic views of the surrounding landscapes. Explore the ruins and imagine the castle's rich history.

Assos Village: Stroll through the picturesque streets of Assos and immerse yourself in its romantic atmosphere. Admire the colorful Venetian-style houses, quaint cafes, and charming squares. The village's relaxed ambiance makes it an ideal spot to unwind and enjoy the tranquil surroundings.

Assos Beach: Enjoy a leisurely day at Assos Beach, located just a short walk from the village. This beautiful pebble beach is surrounded by lush greenery and offers clear turquoise waters for swimming and sunbathing. Relax on the shore and take in the stunning coastal views.

Tavernas and Cafes: Indulge in the local cuisine by dining at one of the traditional tavernas in Assos. Sample fresh seafood dishes, taste local specialties, and savor a glass of Robola wine, produced from grapes grown in the region. The waterfront tavernas offer a delightful dining experience with scenic views.

Skala

Skala, situated on the southern coast of Kefalonia, is a popular seaside resort known for its long sandy beach, lively atmosphere, and historical sites. Here are some attractions to explore in Skala:

Skala Beach: Skala Beach is one of the largest and most popular beaches in Kefalonia. Stretching for several kilometers, this sandy shore offers crystal-clear waters and plenty of space to relax and soak up the sun. Water sports facilities, beach bars, and restaurants are also available.

Roman Villa: Visit the Roman Villa in Skala, an archaeological site that showcases the remains of a luxurious Roman villa from the 3rd century AD. Explore the well-preserved mosaic floors and admire the intricate designs that depict mythological scenes.

Village of Old Skala: Take a short trip inland to the charming village of Old Skala, where you can experience the traditional side of Kefalonia. Enjoy a leisurely walk through the narrow streets, visit the quaint church, and appreciate the authentic atmosphere of the village.

Mount Ainos National Park: Embark on a scenic drive or hike to Mount Ainos National Park, located near Skala. This protected area is home to the island's highest peak, Mount Ainos, and offers stunning panoramic views, dense forests, and a variety of flora and fauna.

Excursions and Boat Tours: Skala serves as a starting point for various boat tours and excursions to neighboring islands or secluded beaches. Consider joining a boat trip to explore the nearby coastline, visit the neighboring island of Ithaca, or enjoy snorkeling in crystal-clear waters.

Exploring Assos and Skala allows you to witness the beauty and diversity of Kefalonia's coastal regions. Whether it's the historical charm of Assos or the vibrant seaside atmosphere of Skala, these destinations offer memorable experiences that highlight the island's allure.

Poros

Poros, located on the southeastern coast of Kefalonia, is a picturesque village known for its scenic harbor, traditional charm, and tranquil atmosphere. Here are some attractions to explore in Poros:

Poros Beach: Start your visit by enjoying the sandy shores of Poros Beach. This family-friendly beach offers calm waters and is equipped with sunbeds and umbrellas. Relax, swim, or take a leisurely stroll along the coast.

Poros Port: Take a walk along the charming harbor of Poros, lined with colorful fishing boats and waterfront tavernas. Enjoy a meal or a refreshing drink while admiring the picturesque views of the sea and the surrounding landscapes.

Agios Ioannis Beach: Just a short distance from Poros, you'll find Agios Ioannis Beach, a secluded gem nestled in a small bay. With crystal-clear turquoise waters and a peaceful atmosphere, it's an ideal spot for relaxation and tranquility.

Monastery of Atros: Venture inland to visit the Monastery of Atros, one of the oldest monasteries on Kefalonia. Perched on a hilltop, it offers panoramic views of the surrounding countryside and the sea. Explore the monastery's grounds and admire the Byzantine architecture.

Boat Trips: Consider joining a boat trip from Poros to explore the nearby coastline and discover hidden coves and pristine beaches. Boat tours may also take you to neighboring islands such as Ithaca or Zakynthos, providing an opportunity to explore the wider Ionian Sea.

Agia Efimia

Agia Efimia, located on the northeastern coast of Kefalonia, is a charming village known for its picturesque harbor, traditional architecture, and serene surroundings. Here are some attractions to explore in Agia Efimia:

Agia Efimia Harbor: Begin your visit by strolling along the vibrant harbor of Agia Efimia, adorned with colorful fishing boats and lined with waterfront cafes and tavernas. Enjoy a meal or a cup of coffee while taking in the charming ambiance of the village.

Agia Efimia Beaches: Agia Efimia is surrounded by several beautiful beaches. Explore Myrtos Beach, one of the most famous beaches in Greece, known for its dramatic cliffs and turquoise waters. You can also visit nearby beaches like Kimilia, Alaties, and Antisamos for a variety of seaside experiences.

Myrtos Beach

Melissani Lake: Take a short drive from Agia Efimia to visit the famous Melissani Cave and its underground lake. Embark on a boat tour through the cave's stunning chambers and witness the mesmerizing reflections created by the sunlight filtering through the cave's roof.

Explore the Village: Wander through the streets of Agia Efimia and admire the traditional architecture, with colorful houses and flower-filled courtyards. Explore the local shops, offering handmade crafts, souvenirs, and local products.

Boat Rental: Rent a small motorboat from Agia Efimia's harbor and explore the picturesque bays and hidden beaches along the coastline at your own pace. This gives you the freedom to discover secluded spots and enjoy the tranquil waters of the Ionian Sea.

Exploring Poros and Agia Efimia allows you to uncover the hidden gems and tranquil beauty of Kefalonia's eastern coast. Whether it's the peaceful ambiance of Poros or the traditional charm of Agia Efimia, these destinations offer a delightful blend of natural scenery, coastal delights, and authentic Greek village life.

CHAPTER 4

TOP ATTRACTIONS AND LANDMARKS

Melissani Cave

Melissani Cave, also known as the Melissani Lake Cave, is one of the most captivating natural wonders on the island of Kefalonia. It is an underground lake that has an open ceiling that lights up its blue water.

Here's what makes it a top attraction:

Enchanting Underground Lake: Step into a mesmerizing underground world as you enter Melissani Cave. The cave features a partially collapsed roof, creating an open-air chamber that reveals a stunning turquoise lake below. The sunlight filtering through the opening creates a magical play of light and shadow on the water's surface.

Boat Tour: Take a boat tour to explore the enchanting cave and its crystal-clear lake. Glide across the calm waters as your guide shares fascinating stories and legends associated with the cave. Marvel at the otherworldly beauty of the stalactites and stalagmites that adorn the cave's walls.

Spectacular Lighting Effects: The interplay of natural light and the cave's interior creates a surreal experience. The sun's rays pierce through the opening, illuminating the water and creating dazzling hues of blue and green. The colors and reflections change throughout the day, offering a different visual spectacle with each visit.

Captivating Acoustics: Another notable feature of Melissani Cave is its exceptional acoustics. The unique cave structure enhances sound, making it a popular spot for musical performances and concerts. Experience the magical acoustics firsthand as you listen to the melodies reverberating through the chamber.

Surrounding Scenery: Melissani Cave is nestled in a lush setting, surrounded by verdant forests and striking karst landscape. The cave's location near the village of Karavomilos offers a serene environment, inviting visitors to embrace the natural beauty of Kefalonia.

Melissani Cave's ethereal beauty and its stunning underground lake make it a must-visit attraction on the island. The combination of the captivating lighting effects, the boat tour experience, and the surrounding scenic landscapes create an unforgettable journey into a subterranean world of wonder.

Assos Village and Castle

The charming village of Assos, nestled on a scenic peninsula in Kefalonia, is a picturesque destination that exudes tranquility and historical charm. The village is famous for its captivating setting and its crowning jewel, the Assos Castle. Here's what makes Assos Village and Castle a must-visit:

Assos Village

Traditional Ambiance: As you approach Assos, you'll be captivated by its traditional ambiance. The village features colorful Venetian-style houses adorned with vibrant flowers, creating a postcard-perfect scene. Take a leisurely stroll through its narrow streets and soak in the authentic atmosphere.

Scenic Harbor: Assos is blessed with a picturesque harbor that adds to its allure. The harbor is lined with waterfront tavernas and cafes where you can savor delicious local cuisine while enjoying the captivating views of the sea and the surrounding landscapes.

Serene Atmosphere: Assos offers a peaceful and laid-back atmosphere, perfect for those seeking a tranquil escape. The village's small size and remote location contribute to its serene ambiance, allowing visitors to relax and immerse themselves in the natural beauty of the area.

Traditional Tavernas: Indulge in the local culinary delights at the traditional tavernas in Assos. Sample freshly caught seafood, taste local specialties like moussaka and souvlaki, and complement your meal with a glass of regional wine. The village's tavernas offer a delightful dining experience infused with warm Greek hospitality.

Assos Castle

Historical Landmark: Dominating the peninsula, the Assos Castle stands as a testament to the island's rich history. The castle dates back to the 16th century and offers a glimpse into the Venetian era. Explore the castle's ruins, climb its walls, and admire the panoramic views of the surrounding sea and landscape.

Scenic Hiking Trails: Embark on a hiking adventure to reach the Assos Castle. The trail meanders through lush vegetation and offers stunning vistas along the way. The hike provides a rewarding experience, allowing you to appreciate the natural beauty of Kefalonia while discovering the historical significance of the castle.

Panoramic Views: Upon reaching the summit of the castle, you'll be rewarded with panoramic views that stretch as far as the eye can see. Feast your eyes on the azure Ionian Sea, the rugged coastline, and the charming village below. The vistas from the castle create a remarkable backdrop for memorable photographs.

Assos Village and Castle combine natural beauty, historical significance, and traditional charm, making them an essential part of any visit to Kefalonia. Whether you're immersing yourself in the village's relaxed ambiance, savoring local cuisine, or exploring the remnants of the impressive castle, Assos promises an enchanting experience that will leave a lasting impression.

Mount Ainos National Park

Mount Ainos National Park, located in the heart of Kefalonia, is a natural paradise that showcases the island's diverse flora, fauna, and breathtaking landscapes. Mount Ainos is the tallest mountain in Kefalonia. Here's what makes Mount Ainos National Park a must-visit destination:

Majestic Mountain Peak: At the heart of the national park stands Mount Ainos, the highest peak on Kefalonia. The mountain reaches an elevation of 1,628 meters (5,341 feet) and offers awe-inspiring panoramic views of the surrounding countryside, coastline, and the Ionian Sea. Hiking to the summit provides a rewarding experience for outdoor enthusiasts and nature lovers.

Dense Forests: Mount Ainos is renowned for its dense forests, which are predominantly covered in Kefalonian fir trees, a species unique to the island. As you explore the park's trails, you'll find yourself immersed in a lush green world, surrounded by the scents and sounds of nature.

Biodiversity: Mount Ainos National Park is home to a rich variety of plant and animal species. The park's diverse ecosystems support a range of wildlife, including wild horses, foxes, and various bird species. Keep an eye out for rare orchids and other endemic plants that flourish in the park's protected environment.

Hiking and Nature Trails: The park offers an extensive network of hiking and nature trails, allowing visitors to explore its natural wonders. Embark on a hike through the forests, following well-marked paths that lead you to scenic viewpoints and hidden gems. The trails cater to different fitness levels, offering options for leisurely walks or more challenging treks.

Environmental Education: Mount Ainos National Park also serves as an educational hub, providing insights into the island's unique ecosystems and promoting environmental conservation. Visitors can learn about the park's flora, fauna, and the ongoing efforts to preserve its natural beauty through informative displays and guided tours.

Picnic Areas: The park features designated picnic areas where visitors can take a break, enjoy a meal surrounded by nature, and soak in the peaceful ambiance. These spots provide the perfect opportunity to relax, unwind, and appreciate the tranquility of the park.

Mount Ainos National Park offers a tranquil retreat and a chance to connect with the island's natural heritage. Whether you're hiking to the mountain's summit, exploring its forests, or simply immersing yourself in the serenity of the park, a visit to Mount Ainos promises a memorable experience that celebrates the beauty of Kefalonia's natural landscapes.

Lighthouse of Saint Theodoroi

Saint Theodore Lighthouse

The Lighthouse of Saint Theodoroi, located near Fiscardo on the northern tip of Kefalonia, is a historic landmark that adds to the charm of the island's coastline. Here's what makes the Lighthouse of Saint Theodoroi a noteworthy attraction:

Scenic Location: Perched on a rocky outcrop overlooking the Ionian Sea, the Lighthouse of Saint Theodoroi boasts a stunning location with panoramic views of the coastline. The picturesque setting provides a perfect vantage point to admire the azure waters, rugged cliffs, and the surrounding natural beauty.

Historical Significance: The lighthouse holds historical significance as it has been guiding ships and ensuring safe navigation along the northern coast of Kefalonia for many decades. Its presence is a testament to the island's maritime heritage and serves as a reminder of the importance of maritime safety.

Architectural Charm: The Lighthouse of Saint Theodoroi features a traditional architectural style that reflects the island's cultural heritage. Its whitewashed exterior, complemented by vibrant blue accents, showcases the classic aesthetics commonly associated with Greek lighthouses.

Panoramic Views: Climbing up to the lighthouse provides visitors with breathtaking panoramic views of the surrounding sea and landscape. From the vantage point of the lighthouse, you can gaze out over the vast expanse of the Ionian Sea, admire the neighboring islands, and witness stunning sunsets that paint the sky with vibrant colors.

Photography Opportunities: The Lighthouse of Saint Theodoroi offers excellent opportunities for photography enthusiasts. Capture the picturesque scenery, the contrasting colors of the sea and the lighthouse, and the dramatic coastal cliffs. The lighthouse serves as a striking focal point for stunning photographs.

Coastal Exploration: While visiting the lighthouse, take the opportunity to explore the rugged coastline around Fiscardo. Discover hidden coves, secluded beaches, and rocky cliffs that showcase the raw beauty of Kefalonia's northern shores.

The Lighthouse of Saint Theodoroi stands as a symbol of Kefalonia's maritime heritage and offers a scenic escape for visitors seeking stunning views and a connection to the island's coastal landscapes. Whether you're admiring the lighthouse from afar or standing at its base, it's an attraction that adds to the allure of the island's northern coastline.

Katavothres Sinkholes

The Katavothres Sinkholes, located near Argostoli in Kefalonia, are a fascinating natural phenomenon that has intrigued visitors for many years. Here's what makes the Katavothres Sinkholes a unique and intriguing attraction:

Mysterious Water Disappearance: The Katavothres Sinkholes are known for their peculiar phenomenon where seawater mysteriously disappears into the ground. These sinkholes act as natural funnels that lead the seawater into underground channels, creating a mesmerizing spectacle.

Geological Wonder: The sinkholes are a result of the island's geological formations, which consist of porous limestone. The underground channels formed by the sinkholes extend for several kilometers beneath the island, leading to a captivating underground world that remains largely unexplored.

Enchanting Sunset Views: The Katavothres Sinkholes offer a picturesque setting to witness breathtaking sunsets. As the sun descends on the horizon, the sky is bathed in vibrant hues of orange, pink, and purple, casting a magical glow over the sinkholes and the surrounding area.

Historical Importance: The Katavothres Sinkholes hold historical significance as they were once part of a hydro-powered mill system. In the past, the water's force was harnessed to power the mills, providing energy for various industrial purposes. The remnants of the mills can still be seen near the sinkholes.

Geological and Hydrological Research: The sinkholes have attracted the attention of scientists and researchers, who have studied the unique hydrological phenomenon and the geological characteristics of the area. Exploring the sinkholes provides an opportunity to learn about the island's geological history and the intricate underground water systems.

Coastal Promenade: A coastal promenade has been developed around the sinkholes, allowing visitors to enjoy a leisurely walk or bike ride while taking in the beautiful coastal scenery. The promenade provides stunning views of the sinkholes and the sparkling Ionian Sea.

The Katavothres Sinkholes offer a blend of natural beauty, geological wonder, and historical significance. Witnessing the seawater disappearing into the sinkholes, admiring the enchanting sunsets, and exploring the coastal promenade all contribute to a memorable experience that showcases the unique character of Kefalonia's landscapes.

Monastery of Agios Gerasimos

The Monastery of Agios Gerasimos, located near the village of Valsamata in Kefalonia, is a significant religious and cultural site that holds deep reverence among the locals. Here's what makes the Monastery of Agios Gerasimos a revered and remarkable attraction:

Spiritual Significance: The monastery is dedicated to Saint Gerasimos, the patron saint of Kefalonia. Saint Gerasimos is highly venerated by the island's residents, who believe in his miraculous powers and seek his intercession for healing and protection. The monastery serves as a place of pilgrimage and worship for both locals and visitors.

Saint Gerasimos' Tomb: The monastery is home to the tomb of Saint Gerasimos, which is considered a sacred and revered site. Pilgrims often visit the tomb to pay their respects and seek blessings from the saint. The tomb is adorned with religious icons and candles, creating a solemn and spiritual ambiance.

Byzantine Architecture: The Monastery of Agios Gerasimos showcases traditional Byzantine architecture with its stone walls, red-tiled roofs, and elegant bell tower. The interior features beautiful frescoes, intricate woodwork, and ornate religious icons, providing a glimpse into the island's rich artistic and architectural heritage.

Monastic Life: The monastery is an active monastic community where monks and nuns reside and lead a contemplative way of life. Visitors can witness the daily rituals and prayers conducted by the resident monks, offering a unique glimpse into the monastic traditions of Kefalonia.

Religious Festivals: Throughout the year, the Monastery of Agios Gerasimos hosts religious festivals and celebrations, attracting pilgrims from all over the island. These festivities are marked by processions, liturgies, and traditional customs, offering a vibrant and immersive experience of the island's religious traditions.

A visit to the Monastery of Agios Gerasimos offers a unique opportunity to connect with the island's spiritual heritage, witness the devoutness of the locals, and appreciate the beauty of Byzantine art and architecture.

Monastery of Agios Gerasimos

CHAPTER 5

BEACHES AND COASTAL GEMS

Xi Beach

Xi Beach

Xi Beach, situated on the southern coast of Kefalonia, is a unique and stunning beach that captivates visitors with its distinctive features. Here's what makes Xi Beach a must-visit coastal gem:

Reddish Sand and Clay Cliffs: Xi Beach is known for its reddish-hued sand, which contrasts beautifully with the turquoise waters of the Ionian Sea. The sand is mixed with clay, creating a soft and velvety texture that visitors enjoy applying as a natural spa treatment. The beach is also flanked by striking clay cliffs, adding to its allure.

Shallow and Calm Waters: The waters of Xi Beach are generally shallow and calm, making it a popular choice for families with children and those who prefer gentle swimming conditions. The gradual slope of the seabed allows for easy access and creates a safe environment for leisurely bathing and water activities.

Water Sports: Xi Beach offers a range of water sports activities for those seeking a bit of adventure. Jet skiing, paddleboarding, and banana boat rides are among the popular options available. Experience the thrill of gliding across the surface of the sea or test your balance on a stand-up paddleboard.

Beach Facilities: Xi Beach is well-equipped with amenities to enhance your beach experience. Sunbeds and umbrellas are available for rent, providing comfort and shade for sunbathers. Beachside tavernas and bars offer refreshments and delicious meals, allowing you to savor local cuisine and cool off with a refreshing drink.

Natural Surroundings: While visiting Xi Beach, take a moment to appreciate the natural beauty that surrounds it. The beach is backed by lush green hills, creating a serene and scenic backdrop. You can also explore the nearby countryside, which is dotted with olive groves and traditional villages, providing a glimpse into the island's rural charm.

Sunset Views: Xi Beach offers breathtaking sunset views, as the sun dips below the horizon, casting a warm glow over the sandy shores and the sea. Witnessing the vivid colors and the tranquil ambiance during sunset creates a magical and romantic atmosphere.

Xi Beach's distinctive features, from its reddish sand and clay cliffs to its calm waters and water sports opportunities, make it a standout destination on Kefalonia's coastline. Whether you're seeking relaxation, family-friendly fun, or picturesque sunsets, Xi Beach promises a memorable experience that showcases the island's natural beauty.

Makris Gialos Beach

Makris Gialos Beach, located on the southern coast of Kefalonia, is a renowned and picturesque beach that offers visitors a delightful coastal experience. Here's what makes Makris Gialos Beach a must-visit destination:

Golden Sands and Crystal-Clear Waters: Makris Gialos Beach is known for its long stretch of golden sand and crystal-clear turquoise waters. The soft sand invites sunbathers to relax and soak up the sun, while the inviting waters beckon swimmers to take a refreshing dip. The pristine conditions of the beach make it an ideal spot for leisurely beach activities.

Blue Flag Beach: Makris Gialos Beach has been awarded the prestigious Blue Flag designation, indicating its high standards of cleanliness, safety, and environmental management. Visitors can enjoy the beach with peace of mind, knowing that it meets strict criteria for water quality and environmental sustainability.

Water Sports and Activities: Makris Gialos Beach offers a range of water sports and activities to cater to adventure seekers. Jet skiing, parasailing, and banana boat rides are among the popular options available. Embark on an exhilarating ride across the waves or soar above the beach for an adrenaline-pumping experience.

Beachside Facilities: The beach is well-equipped with facilities to enhance your visit. Sunbeds and umbrellas are available for rent, providing comfort and shade for sunbathers. There are also beachside tavernas and bars where you can indulge in delicious snacks, refreshing drinks, and traditional Greek cuisine.

Stunning Coastal Scenery: The surroundings of Makris Gialos Beach are simply breathtaking. The beach is framed by rugged cliffs and verdant hills, creating a stunning backdrop that adds to its natural beauty. Take a moment to appreciate the panoramic views and the harmonious blend of land, sea, and sky.

Sunset Splendor: As the day draws to a close, Makris Gialos Beach offers a magical setting to witness captivating sunsets. The sky transforms into a palette of warm colors, casting a golden glow over the beach and creating a romantic ambiance. It's a perfect moment to unwind and appreciate the beauty of nature.

Makris Gialos Beach's golden sands, clear waters, water sports options, and stunning scenery make it an exceptional coastal gem on Kefalonia. Whether you're seeking relaxation, adventure, or scenic views, a visit to this beach promises a memorable experience that celebrates the island's natural beauty.

Petani Beach

Petani Beach, situated on the northwestern coast of Kefalonia, is a hidden gem that showcases the island's natural beauty and offers a tranquil escape for beach lovers. Here's what makes Petani Beach a must-visit destination:

Pristine Beauty: Petani Beach is renowned for its pristine beauty and unspoiled surroundings. The beach boasts a long stretch of fine white pebbles and crystal-clear turquoise waters, creating a picturesque and idyllic setting. The unspoiled nature of Petani Beach adds to its charm, providing a serene and tranquil atmosphere.

Dramatic Cliffside Setting: The beach is nestled beneath dramatic limestone cliffs, adding to its allure and creating a sense of seclusion. The towering cliffs offer a stunning backdrop and provide natural shade during certain times of the day, making it a comfortable spot to relax and enjoy the beach.

Swimming and Snorkeling: The calm and inviting waters of Petani Beach make it ideal for swimming and snorkeling. The crystal-clear sea allows for excellent visibility, enabling you to discover the underwater world teeming with marine life. Explore the vibrant reefs and swim in the refreshing waters for a memorable aquatic experience.

Panoramic Views: As you approach Petani Beach, you'll be treated to panoramic views that are simply breathtaking. From various vantage points along the coast, you can admire the expansive sea, the sweeping beach, and the verdant hills that encompass the area. The vistas provide a sense of tranquility and natural splendor.

Beachside Tavernas: Petani Beach is complemented by a few tavernas offering delightful dining options. Indulge in fresh seafood, traditional Greek dishes, and local delicacies while taking in the stunning views of the beach and the surrounding landscapes. The beachside tavernas provide a perfect setting for a leisurely meal.

Sunset Serenity: Petani Beach offers a romantic setting to witness the beauty of a Kefalonian sunset. As the sun sinks below the horizon, the sky transforms into a canvas of vibrant colors, casting a warm glow over the beach and creating a serene and enchanting atmosphere.

Petani Beach's natural beauty, tranquil ambiance, and stunning surroundings make it a hidden paradise on Kefalonia's northwestern coast. Whether you're seeking relaxation, underwater exploration, or simply the pleasure of admiring breathtaking views, a visit to Petani Beach promises an unforgettable experience immersed in the island's coastal splendor.

Antisamos Beach

Antisamos Beach, located near Sami on the eastern coast of Kefalonia, is a captivating and scenic beach that enchants visitors with its azure waters and lush surroundings. Here's what makes Antisamos Beach a must-visit destination:

Crystal-Clear Waters: Antisamos Beach is renowned for its crystal-clear that invites visitors to take a refreshing swim or snorkel. The pristine conditions of the sea allow for excellent visibility, revealing a vibrant underwater world teeming with marine life and colorful reefs.

Dramatic Landscape: The beach is nestled between steep, verdant hills, creating a dramatic and picturesque landscape. The lush greenery serves as a stunning backdrop to the sparkling sea, adding to the beach's natural beauty and creating a sense of tranquility and seclusion.

Soft Pebble Shore: Antisamos Beach features a soft pebble shore that offers a comfortable surface for sunbathing and relaxing. The smooth pebbles provide a unique texture underfoot and contribute to the beach's distinctive charm. Sun loungers and umbrellas are available for rent, ensuring a comfortable beach experience.

Water Sports Activities: For those seeking adventure, Antisamos Beach offers a range of water sports activities. Try your hand at kayaking, paddleboarding, or even windsurfing to make the most of the beach's dynamic environment. Engaging in water sports provides a thrilling way to experience the beauty of the sea.

Scenic Walking Trails: Surrounding Antisamos Beach are scenic walking trails that wind through the hills and offer stunning viewpoints of the coastline. Embark on a leisurely hike to explore the natural wonders and enjoy panoramic vistas that showcase the harmony of land and sea.

Beachside Amenities: The beach is well-equipped with amenities to ensure a pleasant visit. There are beachside tavernas and cafes where you can savor traditional Greek cuisine and enjoy refreshing drinks. Facilities such as showers and changing rooms are also available for your convenience.

Antisamos Beach's pristine waters, striking landscape, and range of activities make it an alluring coastal gem on Kefalonia's eastern coast.

Emblisi Beach

Emblisi Beach, situated near Fiscardo on the northern coast of Kefalonia, is a hidden gem that offers visitors a peaceful and picturesque coastal escape. Here's what makes Emblisi Beach a must-visit destination:

Secluded and Serene: Emblisi Beach exudes a tranquil and secluded ambiance, making it an ideal spot for those seeking a peaceful retreat. The beach is tucked away in a sheltered cove, surrounded by lush greenery and dramatic cliffs, creating a serene environment that invites relaxation and tranquility.

Pristine Waters and Soft Sand: The crystal-clear waters of Emblisi Beach are inviting and perfect for swimming. The calm sea allows for a refreshing dip, and the soft sand provides a comfortable surface for sunbathing and leisurely walks along the shore. Enjoy the gentle lapping of the waves as you unwind and soak up the sun.

Natural Scenic Beauty: The beach's natural beauty is captivating, with its rugged cliffs, clear turquoise waters, and the verdant hills that envelop the area. The picturesque scenery provides a feast for the eyes and offers plenty of opportunities for stunning photographs and moments of appreciation.

Snorkeling and Exploring: The underwater world around Emblisi Beach is rich in marine life, making it an excellent spot for snorkeling. Dive beneath the surface and discover colorful fish, vibrant reefs, and the fascinating marine ecosystem. Explore the hidden corners of the sea and embrace the sense of adventure.

Walking Trails: Emblisi Beach is surrounded by scenic walking trails that wind through the hills, offering breathtaking viewpoints of the coastline. Embark on a leisurely hike to explore the natural wonders, immerse yourself in the captivating landscapes, and enjoy the serenity of the area.

Authentic Greek Tavernas: Nearby, in the charming village of Fiscardo, you'll find authentic Greek tavernas where you can savor delicious local cuisine. After a day of beach relaxation, indulge in fresh seafood, traditional Greek dishes, and regional delicacies while enjoying the warm hospitality of the local establishments.

Emblisi Beach's secluded charm, pristine waters, and breathtaking surroundings make it a hidden paradise on Kefalonia's northern coast.

Myrtos Beach

CHAPTER 6

OUTDOOR ADVENTURES AND ACTIVITIES

Hiking and Nature Trails

Kefalonia offers a plethora of hiking and nature trails that allow you to explore the island's natural wonders and appreciate its diverse landscapes. Here's what makes hiking in Kefalonia an exciting outdoor adventure:

Varied Terrain: Kefalonia's hiking trails traverse a variety of terrains, including lush forests, rugged coastlines, and rolling hills. Whether you prefer leisurely walks or more challenging hikes, there are trails suitable for every fitness level and interest.

Mount Ainos National Park: A highlight for hikers is Mount Ainos National Park, where you can embark on rewarding hikes to the island's highest peak. Explore the park's dense forests, marvel at the unique flora and fauna, and enjoy panoramic views of the surrounding landscapes.

Scenic Coastal Paths: Along the coastline, there are stunning coastal paths that offer breathtaking views of the sea and cliffs. Hike along the rugged trails, discover hidden coves, and capture the beauty of the dramatic coastlines that Kefalonia is renowned for.

Melissani Cave to Karavomilos: Take a leisurely walk from Melissani Cave to the village of Karavomilos, following a scenic path that winds through picturesque landscapes. Immerse yourself in the natural beauty of the area while enjoying the tranquility of the surroundings.

Water Sports and Diving

Kefalonia's crystal-clear waters and diverse marine life make it a paradise for water sports enthusiasts and diving enthusiasts alike. Here's what you can experience in terms of water sports and diving on the island:

Kayaking and Paddleboarding: Explore the coastline at your own pace by kayaking or paddleboarding. Navigate the calm waters, discover hidden coves, and enjoy a unique perspective of Kefalonia's stunning landscapes.

Jet Skiing and Waterskiing: For those seeking a thrill, jet skiing and waterskiing are popular water sports activities on the island. Feel the rush of adrenaline as you zip across the waves and experience the excitement of these high-speed water adventures.

Snorkeling and Diving: Discover the vibrant underwater world surrounding Kefalonia through snorkeling and diving. Dive beneath the surface to explore colorful reefs, encounter a variety of marine species, and witness the beauty of the Mediterranean sea life.

Wine Tours and Tasting

Kefalonia's rich soil and favorable climate provide the perfect conditions for vineyards to flourish, making wine tours and tasting experiences a delightful activity on the island. Here's what you can expect from wine tours and tastings in Kefalonia:

Vineyard Visits: Embark on guided tours of Kefalonia's vineyards, where you can explore the lush vine rows and learn about the local grape varieties. Discover the winemaking process, from grape cultivation to wine production, while enjoying the scenic beauty of the vineyard landscapes.

Wine Tastings: Indulge in wine tastings that allow you to savor a variety of Kefalonia's exquisite wines. Sample the island's renowned Robola wine, a crisp white wine with citrus notes, as well as other regional varietals. Learn about the characteristics and flavors of each wine, and gain insights into the island's winemaking traditions.

Food Pairings: Enhance your wine tasting experience with delectable food pairings. Many wineries in Kefalonia offer local cheeses, olives, and traditional Greek delicacies that complement the wines perfectly. Immerse yourself in the culinary delights of the island as you enjoy the harmonious marriage of flavors.

Wine Festivals and Events: Time your visit to Kefalonia with one of the island's wine festivals or events. These celebrations showcase the best of Kefalonian wines, featuring live music, cultural performances, and an opportunity to mingle with local winemakers.

Olive Oil Experiences

Kefalonia is known for its high-quality olive oil, and exploring olive oil experiences on the island allows you to appreciate this culinary treasure. Here's what you can enjoy when it comes to olive oil experiences in Kefalonia:

Olive Grove Tours: Take guided tours through Kefalonia's olive groves, where you can witness the ancient olive trees and learn about the olive oil production process. Discover the cultivation techniques, the harvesting methods, and the traditional practices that contribute to the island's exceptional olive oil.

Olive Oil Tastings: Engage in olive oil tastings to sample the different flavors and aromas of Kefalonia's olive oils. Learn how to identify the unique characteristics of high-quality olive oil, from its color and viscosity to its taste and aftertaste. Expand your knowledge and appreciation of this prized culinary ingredient.

Cooking Classes: Join cooking classes that focus on using olive oil as a key ingredient in traditional Greek cuisine. Learn how to prepare classic dishes and discover the importance of olive oil in enhancing flavors and promoting a healthy Mediterranean diet. Immerse yourself in the culinary traditions of Kefalonia.

Olive Oil Festivals: Experience the lively atmosphere of olive oil festivals that celebrate the island's olive oil production. These festivals feature tastings, cultural events, and demonstrations of traditional olive oil processing techniques. Immerse yourself in the vibrant ambiance and discover the significance of olive oil in Kefalonia's culture.

Engaging in wine tours and tastings, as well as olive oil experiences, allows you to savor the flavors of Kefalonia and immerse yourself in the island's culinary heritage.

Asos Castle

CHAPTER 7

GASTRONOMY AND CULINARY DELIGHTS

Traditional Kefalonian Cuisine

Kefalonia's culinary scene is rich with traditional flavors and delightful dishes that showcase the island's gastronomic heritage. Here's an overview of traditional Kefalonian cuisine:

Robola Wine: Kefalonia is renowned for its Robola wine, a crisp and refreshing white wine made from the Robola grape variety. Enjoy a glass of this local wine, known for its citrusy notes and distinctive character, as you explore the island's culinary offerings.

Kefalonian Meat Pie (Kreatopita): This savory pie is a beloved dish in Kefalonia. It consists of layers of tender meat, usually beef or lamb, mixed with onions, garlic, herbs, and spices. The filling is encased in a flaky pastry crust, creating a satisfying and flavorsome delicacy.

Seafood Delights: As an island, Kefalonia boasts an abundance of fresh seafood. Sample dishes such as grilled octopus, marinated anchovies (gavros marinatos), or the local specialty called bourdeto—a spicy fish stew cooked with red pepper and tomato sauce.

Kefalonian Meat Sausage (Loukaniko): Made with a combination of pork and spices, Kefalonian loukaniko is a traditional sausage bursting with rich flavors. Grilled or fried, it is often served as an appetizer or alongside other meat dishes.

Riganada: This rustic dish features toasted bread topped with a mixture of tomato, onion, garlic, and herbs, drizzled with olive oil. Riganada is a simple yet delicious appetizer that highlights the fresh flavors of Kefalonian ingredients.

Local Ingredients and Dishes

Kefalonia's cuisine showcases the island's abundance of local ingredients and traditional dishes. Here are some notable ingredients and dishes to explore:

Olive Oil: Kefalonia produces exceptional olive oil, known for its high quality and distinctive taste. This golden elixir is an essential ingredient in Kefalonian cuisine, adding richness and flavor to various dishes.

Feta Cheese: The tangy and creamy feta cheese of Kefalonia is a staple in the island's cuisine. Enjoy it in traditional Greek salads, as a topping for savory pies, or paired with fresh fruits and honey for a delightful combination of flavors.

Honey: Kefalonia's honey is renowned for its rich taste and aromatic qualities. Try it drizzled over yogurt, as a sweetener in pastries, or as a complement to cheese for a delightful blend of flavors.

Kefalonian Meat and Dairy: Kefalonia is known for its high-quality meat and dairy products. Sample dishes featuring locally sourced lamb, goat, and pork, along with traditional cheeses like kefalotyri and ladotyri.

Must-Try Restaurants and Tavernas

When exploring Kefalonia's culinary scene, be sure to visit these must-try restaurants and tavernas:

Fiskardo: Located in the charming village of Fiscardo, this picturesque harbor is dotted with tavernas and restaurants serving fresh seafood dishes. Indulge in the catch of the day while enjoying stunning views of the waterfront.

Fiskardo

Argostoli: The capital city of Kefalonia, Argostoli, offers a wide range of dining options. Explore the city's bustling central square and side streets to discover tavernas serving traditional Kefalonian cuisine, from hearty meat dishes to delectable seafood platters.

Assos: Nestled on a scenic peninsula, the village of Assos is home to waterfront tavernas offering a relaxing ambiance and captivating views. Enjoy a leisurely meal while taking in the beauty of the surrounding landscapes.

Lixouri: Cross over to the western coast of Kefalonia to find charming tavernas in the town of Lixouri. Sample local specialties and embrace the warm hospitality of this laid-back destination.

Traditional Mountain Villages: Venture into the island's traditional mountain villages, such as Makriotika and Valsamata, where you can savor authentic Kefalonian dishes in rustic tavernas. These hidden gems provide a glimpse into the island's traditional way of life and culinary traditions.

Sweet Treats and Desserts

Kefalonia is known for its delectable sweet treats and desserts that showcase the island's culinary creativity. Here are some must-try sweet treats in Kefalonia:

Pasteli: This traditional Greek treat consists of sesame seeds bound together with honey, creating a delightful combination of crunchiness and sweetness. Pasteli is a popular snack to enjoy throughout the day.

Mandola: These almond-based cookies are a specialty of Kefalonia. Made with ground almonds, sugar, and egg whites, they are shaped into crescents and baked to golden perfection. Mandola cookies are perfect for those with a sweet tooth.

Mandoles: Mandoles are caramelized almonds coated in a thin layer of dark chocolate, creating a heavenly blend of sweet and nutty flavors. They make for a delicious treat or a delightful gift to take home.

Kefalonian Cake (Kefalonitiki Tarta): This traditional cake is a decadent dessert made with layers of sponge cake, almond paste, and a sweet cinnamon-spiced syrup. It is often topped with powdered sugar and accompanied by a scoop of vanilla ice cream.

Coffee Culture in Kefalonia

Coffee culture holds a special place in Kefalonia, with numerous cafes and coffee houses dotting the island. Here's what you can expect when it comes to coffee culture in Kefalonia:

Greek Coffee: Start your day like the locals with a cup of traditional Greek coffee. Brewed in a traditional brass pot, Greek coffee is strong and flavorful. Enjoy it in a traditional cafe while soaking up the laid-back atmosphere.

Freddo Espresso: Embrace the island's warm climate with a refreshing Freddo Espresso. This iced coffee is made by shaking espresso with ice, creating a cool and invigorating beverage that provides a much-needed respite from the summer heat.

Frappé: Another popular chilled coffee drink in Kefalonia is the Frappé. Made by blending instant coffee with ice and water, and sweetened to taste, it is a perfect choice for a midday pick-me-up.

Traditional Coffee Houses: Explore the traditional coffee houses in Kefalonia, where you can savor your coffee alongside traditional Greek pastries and sweets. These cozy establishments often offer a glimpse into the island's cultural heritage and provide a welcoming ambiance to relax and socialize.

Immerse yourself in Kefalonia's gastronomic delights by exploring its vineyards, indulging in sweet treats, and embracing the island's coffee culture.

CHAPTER 8

FESTIVALS AND EVENTS

Religious Festivals and Processions

Religious festivals and processions play an important role in the cultural fabric of Kefalonia, allowing locals and visitors to experience the island's religious heritage. Here are some notable religious festivals and processions in Kefalonia:

Feast of Agios Gerasimos: The Feast of Agios Gerasimos, the patron saint of Kefalonia, is celebrated on August 16th. Pilgrims from all over the island and beyond gather at the Monastery of Agios Gerasimos to pay homage to the saint, participate in religious ceremonies, and seek blessings.

Holy Week and Easter: Holy Week and Easter are significant religious observances in Kefalonia. Various processions and religious ceremonies take place throughout the island, with the culmination being the midnight

Resurrection service and the joyous celebration of Easter Sunday.

Panagia Fidousa: The festival of Panagia Fidousa is celebrated on August 15th. Devotees gather at the Church of Panagia Fidousa in Markopoulo to honor the Virgin Mary. The celebrations include religious services, processions, and traditional festivities.

Assumption of the Virgin Mary: On August 15th, the Assumption of the Virgin Mary is celebrated across the island. Churches hold special services and processions to commemorate the ascent of the Virgin Mary into heaven.

These religious festivals and processions provide an opportunity to witness the deep-rooted religious traditions of Kefalonia, experience the island's cultural heritage, and engage in the community celebrations that bring together locals and visitors alike.

Music and Cultural Events

Kefalonia hosts a variety of music and cultural events throughout the year, offering a vibrant and enriching experience for locals and visitors alike. Here's what you can expect from music and cultural events in Kefalonia:

Traditional Music Performances: Experience the soul-stirring sounds of traditional Kefalonian music through live performances. Local musicians and music groups showcase traditional instruments and melodies, offering a glimpse into the island's rich musical heritage.

Folklore Festivals: Folklore festivals are held in various villages and towns across Kefalonia, celebrating the island's cultural traditions. These events feature music, dance performances, and exhibitions of traditional crafts, allowing you to immerse yourself in the island's folklore and customs.

Art Exhibitions: Kefalonia's art scene comes alive through exhibitions and art shows that showcase the works of local artists. Explore galleries and cultural spaces to discover a diverse range of artistic expressions, including paintings, sculptures, and mixed media installations.

Cultural Workshops: Engage in cultural workshops that offer hands-on experiences in traditional Kefalonian activities. Learn traditional dances, participate in pottery or weaving workshops, or try your hand at Greek cooking classes. These workshops provide a deeper understanding of the island's cultural practices and allow you to connect with local artisans.

Summer Festivals and Concerts

During the summer months, Kefalonia becomes a hub of lively festivals and concerts that draw both locals and tourists. Here are some highlights of Kefalonia's summer festivals and concerts:

Kefalonia Music Days: This annual music festival brings together renowned musicians from Greece and around the world. Enjoy a variety of musical genres, from classical and jazz to contemporary and traditional, performed in picturesque settings across the island.

Cultural Summer Festivals: Various towns and villages in Kefalonia organize summer festivals featuring live music, dance performances, and theatrical productions. These events create a festive atmosphere, offering a chance to celebrate the arts and enjoy the vibrant energy of the island.

Outdoor Concerts: Open-air concerts are held in scenic locations, such as historic sites, squares, and amphitheaters, providing a unique setting for enjoying live music. From classical symphonies to modern music performances, these concerts offer memorable experiences under the starry Kefalonian sky.

Kefalonia's Independence Day

Kefalonia commemorates its Independence Day on May 21st, celebrating its liberation from Ottoman rule. On this day, various ceremonies and events take place across the island, including:

Flag-Raising Ceremonies: Flag-raising ceremonies are held in towns and villages, where the national flag of Greece is raised in honor of Independence Day. These ceremonies are accompanied by speeches and patriotic songs, fostering a sense of national pride and unity.

Parades and Processions: Colorful parades and processions fill the streets as local schools, marching bands, and community groups participate in the celebrations. Participants proudly display traditional costumes, wave flags, and march to commemorate the island's struggle for independence.

Cultural Events: Cultural events, including music performances, dance presentations, and poetry readings, add to the festive spirit of the day. These events highlight Kefalonia's rich cultural heritage and serve as a reminder of the island's historical significance.

Kefalonia's music and cultural events, summer festivals, and celebrations of Independence Day offer opportunities to immerse yourself in the island's vibrant arts scene, experience its cultural traditions, and celebrate the spirit of Kefalonian identity.

CHAPTER 9

SUGGESTED ITINERARY

Hidden Gems and Off-the-Beaten-Path

Kefalonia is not only known for its popular attractions but also offers hidden gems and off-the-beaten-path destinations that provide unique experiences. Here are some hidden gems in Kefalonia waiting to be discovered:

Platia Ammos Beach: Tucked away on the northern coast, Platia Ammos Beach is a hidden gem accessible only by boat or a steep hike. This secluded beach boasts turquoise waters, fine white sand, and stunning cliffs, offering a tranquil and idyllic setting for relaxation and snorkeling.

Mount Enos: Venture to the heart of Kefalonia and explore Mount Enos, the island's highest peak. With its lush green forests, diverse flora and fauna, and breathtaking vistas, this mountain offers excellent hiking opportunities for nature lovers and outdoor enthusiasts.

Katelios Village: Visit the charming fishing village of Katelios, located on the southern coast of Kefalonia. Known for its laid-back atmosphere, quaint harbor, and traditional tavernas, Katelios offers a glimpse into the island's authentic village life and a chance to enjoy fresh seafood dishes by the sea.

Lighthouse of Saint Theodoroi: Located near Argostoli, the Lighthouse of Saint Theodoroi stands majestically at the edge of a cliff overlooking the Ionian Sea. This picturesque spot offers panoramic views of the coastline and is an ideal place to witness breathtaking sunsets.

Koutavos Lagoon: Explore the Koutavos Lagoon, a tranquil nature reserve situated near Argostoli. Walk along the waterfront promenade, spot various bird species, and enjoy the serenity of this hidden gem, away from the bustling tourist areas.

Drogarati Cave: This cave was discovered many years ago when an earthquake destroyed part of the cave. Discover the stunning Drogarati Cave, an underground wonder featuring impressive stalactite and stalagmite formations. Explore the cavernous chambers, marvel at the acoustics that make it a popular concert venue, and appreciate the beauty of this hidden natural wonder.

Assos Village and Castle: Located on a peninsula, Assos is a picturesque village that exudes charm and tranquility. Wander through its narrow streets, visit the Venetian castle perched on a hilltop, and enjoy breathtaking views of the village and the surrounding turquoise sea.

Exploring these hidden gems and off-the-beaten-path locations allows you to discover the lesser-known aspects of Kefalonia's natural beauty, local culture, and hidden treasures that lie beyond the typical tourist routes.

Itineraries

1-Week Itinerary

Day 1: Arrival and Argostoli

Arrive in Kefalonia and settle into your accommodation.

Spend the day exploring the capital city, Argostoli. Visit the Koutavos Lagoon and walk along the waterfront promenade. Discover the bustling central square, browse local shops, and enjoy a meal at a traditional taverna.

Day 2: Melissani Cave and Karavomilos

Start your day by visiting the enchanting Melissani Cave. Take a boat ride on the underground lake and admire the unique natural formations and stunning blue hues.

Afterward, head to the village of Karavomilos and enjoy a leisurely walk along the scenic path that leads from Melissani Cave to Karavomilos. Take in the beautiful landscapes and enjoy a relaxing lunch by the seaside.

Day 3: Assos and Myrtos Beach

Explore the picturesque village of Assos, known for its charming atmosphere and the Venetian castle perched on a hilltop. Wander through its narrow streets, enjoy panoramic views, and savor a delicious meal at a seaside taverna.

Afterward, visit Myrtos Beach, one of the most famous and beautiful beaches in Kefalonia. Relax on its white pebbles, swim in the crystal-clear waters, and take in the breathtaking scenery.

Day 4: Boat Excursion to Ithaca

Embark on a boat excursion to the neighboring island of Ithaca, legendary home of Odysseus. Explore the island's beautiful bays, hidden coves, and charming villages. Swim in pristine waters, visit the Cave of the Nymphs, and enjoy a traditional Greek lunch on board.

Day 5: Lixouri and Xi Beach

Take a ferry to Lixouri, the second-largest town in Kefalonia. Stroll through its vibrant streets, visit the central square, and sample local delicacies at a taverna.

In the afternoon, head to Xi Beach, known for its unique reddish sand and shallow waters. Relax on the beach, enjoy water sports activities, and treat yourself to a beachside meal.

Day 6: Fiscardo and Emblisi Beach

Visit the charming village of Fiscardo, located in the northern part of the island. Explore its colorful harbor, browse boutique shops, and indulge in fresh seafood at a waterfront taverna.

Afterward, head to Emblisi Beach, a hidden gem with turquoise waters and a tranquil atmosphere. Spend the afternoon swimming, snorkeling, or simply unwinding on the beautiful beach.

Day 7: Mount Ainos and Robola Wine Tasting

Embark on a journey to Mount Ainos National Park. Enjoy a scenic drive to the park and hike to the summit, where you'll be rewarded with panoramic views of the island.

Afterward, visit a local winery to taste the renowned Robola wine. Learn about the winemaking process, sample different varieties, and savor the flavors of Kefalonia's exquisite wines.

This 1-week itinerary allows you to experience the highlights of Kefalonia, from its captivating caves and stunning beaches to its charming villages and rich cultural heritage. However, feel free to adjust the itinerary based on your preferences and available time to make the most of your trip to this beautiful island.

10-Day Itinerary

Day 1: Arrival and Argostoli

Arrive in Kefalonia and settle into your accommodation in Argostoli, the capital city.

Spend the day exploring Argostoli, visiting the Koutavos Lagoon, strolling along the waterfront promenade, and discovering the city's vibrant central square. Enjoy a meal at a traditional taverna and immerse yourself in the local atmosphere.

Day 2: Melissani Cave and Karavomilos

Start your day with a visit to the captivating Melissani Cave. Take a boat ride on the underground lake and admire the stunning natural formations and turquoise waters.

Afterward, head to the nearby village of Karavomilos. Enjoy a leisurely walk along the scenic path that leads from Melissani Cave to Karavomilos, taking in the beautiful landscapes. Have a relaxing lunch by the seaside.

Day 3: Assos and Myrtos Beach

Explore the picturesque village of Assos, known for its charm and the Venetian castle perched on a hilltop. Wander through the narrow streets, soak in the panoramic views, and savor a delicious meal at a seaside taverna.

Afterward, visit Myrtos Beach, one of the most famous and stunning beaches in Kefalonia. Spend the afternoon swimming in the crystal-clear waters and enjoying the breathtaking scenery.

Day 4: Boat Excursion to Ithaca

Embark on a boat excursion to the neighboring island of Ithaca, known as the home of Odysseus. Discover the island's beautiful bays, hidden coves, and charming villages. Swim in pristine waters, visit the Cave of the Nymphs, and enjoy a traditional Greek lunch on board.

Day 5: Lixouri and Xi Beach

Take a ferry to Lixouri, the second-largest town in Kefalonia. Explore its vibrant streets, visit the central square, and indulge in local delicacies at a taverna.

In the afternoon, head to Xi Beach, known for its reddish sand and shallow waters. Relax on the beach, engage in watersports activities, and treat yourself to a beachside meal.

Day 6: Fiscardo and Emblisi Beach

Visit the charming village of Fiscardo, located in the northern part of the island. Explore its colorful harbor, browse boutique shops, and enjoy fresh seafood at a waterfront taverna.

Afterward, head to Emblisi Beach, a hidden gem with turquoise waters and a tranquil atmosphere. Spend the afternoon swimming, snorkeling, or simply unwinding on the beautiful beach.

Day 7: Mount Ainos National Park and Robola Wine Tasting

Embark on a journey to Mount Ainos National Park. Enjoy a scenic drive to the park and hike to the summit, where you'll be rewarded with panoramic views of the island.

Afterward, visit a local winery to taste the renowned Robola wine. Learn about the winemaking process, sample different varieties, and savor the flavors of Kefalonia's exquisite wines.

Day 8: Sami and Antisamos Beach

Explore the town of Sami, known for its charming waterfront and archaeological sites. Visit the Ancient Acropolis of Sami and the Melissani Cave, located nearby.

Spend the afternoon at Antisamos Beach, a picturesque pebble beach surrounded by lush hills. Relax on the beach, swim in the crystal-clear waters, and enjoy the natural beauty of the surroundings.

Day 9: Skala and Mounda Beach

Visit the coastal village of Skala, known for its long sandy beach and vibrant atmosphere. Explore the village, visit the Roman Villa archaeological site, and enjoy a meal at a seaside taverna.

Afterward, head to Mounda Beach, a nesting ground for loggerhead sea turtles. Take a leisurely walk along the beach, admire the protected area, and learn about the conservation efforts in place.

Day 10: Poros and Agia Efimia

Explore the charming coastal village of Poros, known for its picturesque harbor and traditional Greek atmosphere. Stroll along the waterfront, visit the local shops, and enjoy a delicious meal at a seaside taverna.

Afterward, make your way to Agia Efimia, a charming town nestled in a bay. Explore its quaint streets, visit the harbor, and relax with a refreshing drink by the sea.

This 10-day itinerary allows you to fully experience the beauty, culture, and hidden gems of Kefalonia. Feel free to adjust the itinerary based on your preferences and available time to make the most of your trip to this enchanting island.

Family Travel

Traveling with your family to Kefalonia can be a memorable and enjoyable experience. Here are some tips to ensure a smooth and fun-filled trip:

Plan Ahead: Research and plan your itinerary in advance, taking into consideration the interests and needs of every family member. Look for family-friendly accommodations and activities that cater to different age groups.

Pack Wisely: Pack essential items such as sunscreen, hats, insect repellent, comfortable clothing, and any necessary medications. Also, bring along items to keep children entertained during travel, such as books, toys, or portable electronic devices.

Safety First: Ensure the safety of your family by practicing common safety measures. Keep an eye on young children at all times, especially near water or in crowded areas. Familiarize yourself with emergency procedures and have a plan in case of any unforeseen circumstances.

Embrace the Outdoors: Kefalonia offers plenty of outdoor activities for families. Explore beaches, go hiking, or take part in water sports. Enjoy picnics in scenic spots or visit local parks and playgrounds where children can have fun and burn off some energy.

Cultural Immersion: Encourage your children to learn about the local culture and traditions of Kefalonia. Visit historical sites, attend cultural events or festivals, and try traditional food. Engaging in local customs and traditions can be a valuable learning experience for the whole family.

Flexibility and Rest: Remember to pace your itinerary to allow for downtime and rest. Traveling with children can be tiring, so be flexible with your plans and take breaks when needed. Ensure everyone gets enough sleep to keep everyone refreshed and energized throughout the trip.

Child-Friendly Attractions: Kefalonia offers attractions suitable for children, such as water parks, animal sanctuaries, and interactive museums. Research and include these family-friendly attractions in your itinerary to keep children engaged and entertained.

Local Cuisine: Introduce your family to the flavors of Kefalonian cuisine. Let them try traditional dishes and local delicacies. Many restaurants offer children's menus or have options suitable for picky eaters. Embrace the opportunity to broaden their culinary horizons.

Capture Memories: Take plenty of photos and capture the precious moments of your family vacation. Encourage your children to keep a travel journal or scrapbook to document their experiences. These mementos will serve as cherished memories for years to come.

Enjoy Quality Time: The most important aspect of family travel is spending quality time together. Enjoy each other's company, create unforgettable memories, and embrace the opportunity to bond as a family in the beautiful surroundings of Kefalonia.

By following these tips, you can ensure a memorable and enjoyable family vacation in Kefalonia, creating lasting memories that you and your loved ones will treasure.

Kid-Friendly Activities

Kefalonia offers a range of kid-friendly activities that will keep children entertained and engaged during your family vacation. Here are some kid-friendly attractions and experiences in Kefalonia:

Beach Fun: Kefalonia is home to numerous beautiful beaches that are perfect for families. Choose beaches with calm waters and sandy shores, such as Makris Gialos or Lourdas Beach, where children can swim, build sandcastles, and enjoy beach games.

Water Parks: Visit one of the water parks in Kefalonia for a day of splashing fun. The parks feature water slides, pools, and play areas suitable for children of all ages. The Aquatic Water Park in Lixouri and the WaterPark at the Ionian Sea Hotel in Svoronata are popular options.

Animal Encounters: Take your kids to the Kefalonia Wildlife Sense Rescue Center, where they can learn about and interact with rescued animals, including turtles and hedgehogs. It's an educational experience that promotes environmental awareness and conservation.

Caves and Excursions: Explore the magical caves of Kefalonia, such as Melissani Cave and Drogarati Cave. Kids will love the boat rides through the underground lakes and the fascinating rock formations. You can also go on family-friendly boat excursions to discover hidden beaches and snorkeling spots.

Mini Golf: Engage in a friendly game of mini golf at one of the family-friendly mini golf courses on the island. It's a fun activity that allows children to practice their coordination skills while having a great time with the family.

Horseback Riding: Let your kids experience horseback riding in Kefalonia. Several stables offer guided tours and lessons suitable for children, allowing them to connect with nature and enjoy a unique adventure.

Visit a Farm: Take your children to a local farm, such as the Farmland Agritourism in Kefalonia, where they can interact with farm animals, learn about sustainable farming practices, and even participate in activities like milking cows or collecting eggs.

Playground Fun: Visit the local playgrounds in Kefalonia, such as the Kid's Park in Argostoli or the public playgrounds in various towns. Let your children enjoy swings, slides, and other play equipment while making new friends.

Boat Trips and Snorkeling: Join a family-friendly boat trip that includes snorkeling stops. Children can explore the underwater world, spot colorful fish, and swim in clear waters. Many boat trips also provide equipment and guidance for children's safety and enjoyment.

Cooking Classes: Enroll your children in a fun cooking class where they can learn to make traditional Greek dishes. It's a hands-on experience that introduces them to local flavors and culinary traditions.

These kid-friendly activities in Kefalonia ensure that your children have a fantastic time while creating lasting memories. The island's natural beauty, friendly atmosphere, and range of family-oriented attractions make it an ideal destination for a fun-filled family vacation.

CHAPTER 10

Practical Information

Accommodation Options

Kefalonia offers a variety of accommodation options to suit different preferences and budgets. Here are some popular choices:

Hotels and Resorts: Kefalonia has a range of hotels and resorts catering to various needs, from luxury to budget-friendly options. Choose from beachfront resorts with all-inclusive packages, family-friendly hotels with children's facilities, or boutique hotels in charming villages.

Villas and Vacation Rentals: Renting a villa or vacation home is a popular choice for families or larger groups. These accommodations provide more space, privacy, and the flexibility to cook your own meals. Many villas come with private pools and beautiful views of the island.

Apartments and Studios: Apartments and studios are a convenient option for those who prefer a self-catering accommodation experience. These units typically come with a kitchenette or full kitchen facilities, allowing you to prepare your own meals. They are available in various sizes and locations across the island.

Guesthouses and Bed & Breakfasts: For a more intimate and cozy stay, consider booking a guesthouse or bed & breakfast. These accommodations offer a personalized touch, often run by local hosts who can provide insider tips and recommendations. They are perfect for those seeking a more authentic experience.

Camping: If you enjoy the outdoors, camping is an option on Kefalonia. There are several campsites with basic facilities where you can set up tents or park campervans.

Keep in mind that camping is subject to specific regulations, so be sure to check local guidelines.

When choosing accommodation, consider factors such as location, amenities, and proximity to attractions or activities that interest you. It's advisable to book in advance, especially during the peak summer season, to secure your preferred choice.

Whether you prefer a luxurious resort, a cozy villa, or a budget-friendly apartment, Kefalonia offers a range of accommodation options to suit different tastes and requirements.

Best Hotels in Kefalonia

Kefalonia offers a variety of accommodation options to suit different preferences and budgets. Here are some popular choices:

Emelisse Nature Resort: Located near Fiskardo, this luxurious resort offers elegant rooms, stunning sea views, and a private beach. It features excellent amenities such as a spa, infinity pools, and fine dining options.

F Zeen Retreat: Situated in Lourdata, this boutique hotel provides a tranquil and relaxing atmosphere. It offers stylish rooms, a beautiful infinity pool, wellness facilities, and easy access to the beach.

Petani Bay Hotel: Nestled in the picturesque village of Lixouri, this hotel offers panoramic sea views and modern rooms. Guests can enjoy a large swimming pool, a restaurant serving local cuisine, and a peaceful beach nearby.

Apostolata Island Resort & Spa: Located in Skala, this resort provides comfortable rooms, a spa, multiple swimming pools, and breathtaking views of the Ionian Sea. It offers a serene and luxurious retreat for guests.

Mouikis Hotel: Situated in the heart of Argostoli, this centrally located hotel offers clean and comfortable rooms, a rooftop terrace, and easy access to the city's attractions, shops, and restaurants.

How to Budget

Travel Off-Season: Consider visiting Kefalonia during shoulder seasons (spring or autumn) when prices are generally lower compared to the peak summer season. You can find better deals on accommodations and flights during these times.

Book in Advance: Booking your accommodation well in advance can help you secure better rates and availability. Keep an eye out for early booking discounts or package deals that include flights and accommodations.

Self-Catering Options: Opting for self-catering accommodations, such as apartments or villas with kitchen facilities, allows you to save money on dining out. You can prepare some meals using fresh local ingredients from markets or grocery stores.

Explore Local Cuisine: While dining out, try traditional Greek tavernas and local eateries, which often offer delicious and affordable options. Sample local specialties and enjoy the authentic flavors of Kefalonian cuisine without breaking the bank.

Plan Activities Wisely: Research and prioritize the attractions and activities that interest you the most. Some attractions may have entrance fees or additional costs, so planning ahead can help you allocate your budget accordingly.

Use Public Transportation: Kefalonia has a reliable bus network that covers major towns and attractions. Utilizing public transportation can be more cost-effective than renting a car, especially if you're traveling solo or with a small group.

Seek Out Free or Low-Cost Activities: Kefalonia offers many natural attractions and scenic spots that you can enjoy for free, such as beaches, hiking trails, and viewpoints. Take advantage of these opportunities to explore and appreciate the island's beauty without spending much.

By considering these tips, you can manage your budget effectively while enjoying a comfortable stay in Kefalonia. Remember to prioritize your preferences and choose accommodations and activities that align with your budgetary needs.

Transportation Options

Getting There

Getting to this paradise requires careful planning, as Kefalonia offers various transportation options that cater to different preferences and budgets.

Below are the different ways you can reach Kefalonia, ensuring your journey is as smooth and enjoyable as your stay on the island.

Flights: The most convenient and quickest way to reach Kefalonia is by air. The island has its own airport, Kefalonia International Airport (EFL), which is well-connected to major European cities and Greek mainland airports. During the peak season, you'll find regular direct flights from cities like Athens, London, Rome, Frankfurt, and other European hubs. Airlines that operate flights to Kefalonia include Aegean Airlines, Ryanair, EasyJet, and others.

Ferries: If you prefer a more scenic and adventurous route, ferries are a popular choice to reach Kefalonia. The island has several ports that receive ferries from various locations in Greece and Italy. The main ports are Sami, Poros, and Argostoli. Ferries operate from Patras, Astakos, and Killini on the Greek mainland, as well as from neighboring islands such as Zakynthos, Ithaca, and Lefkada. You can choose between standard ferries, which take longer but are more affordable, and high-speed ferries that offer quicker journeys at a slightly higher cost.

Cruise Ships: Kefalonia is also a popular destination for cruise ships, especially during the peak tourist season. Many Mediterranean cruise itineraries include a stop at Kefalonia, allowing travelers to enjoy a day exploring the island's beautiful beaches, villages, and attractions. If you're looking for a more leisurely way to arrive at

Kefalonia and enjoy other destinations along the way, a cruise might be the perfect option for you.

Car Rentals: Once you arrive in Kefalonia, having a car at your disposal will greatly enhance your travel experience. Car rentals are available at the airport, major ports, and in popular tourist areas like Argostoli and Lassi. Having your own vehicle allows you to explore the island at your own pace, visit remote beaches, and discover charming villages tucked away in the hills. However, it's essential to book your rental car in advance, especially during peak season, to ensure availability and competitive prices.

Public Transportation

Kefalonia has a public bus system that connects major towns and villages, making it a cost-effective option for travelers on a budget. Buses are comfortable and reliable, but their schedules might be limited, especially in remote areas. The main bus terminal is in Argostoli, and routes extend to destinations like Lassi, Skala, Fiskardo, and Sami. Keep in mind that if you're planning to explore off-the-beaten-path locations, public transportation may not always be the most convenient option.

Taxis: Taxis are readily available in Kefalonia, offering a convenient mode of transportation, especially for shorter trips or when you prefer not to drive. You can find taxis at the airport, major ports, and in town centers. It's advisable to agree on a fare with the driver before starting your journey, especially for longer trips.

Bicycle Rentals: For the eco-conscious and active travelers, some areas in Kefalonia offer bicycle rentals. Exploring the island by bike can be a rewarding experience, allowing you to get closer to nature and enjoy the island's scenic beauty. However, keep in mind that Kefalonia's terrain can be hilly and challenging, so this option is best suited for experienced cyclists.

Walking and Hiking: If you're an avid walker or hiker, Kefalonia has a plethora of stunning trails to explore. Hiking paths lead to picturesque beaches, lush forests, and panoramic viewpoints, giving you an opportunity to immerse yourself fully in the island's natural wonders. Just be sure to bring appropriate footwear, water, and snacks, as some hikes can be demanding.

In conclusion, getting to Kefalonia is an adventure in itself, with transportation options ranging from flights and ferries to cruises and public buses. The choice you make will depend on your preferences, budget, and time constraints. Once on the island, having a car at your disposal can enhance your travel experience, allowing you to explore Kefalonia's hidden gems at your own pace.

Language and Useful Phrases

The official language of Kefalonia, as well as the rest of Greece, is Greek. While many people in tourist areas speak English, it's always helpful to learn a few basic Greek phrases to enhance your travel experience. Here are some useful phrases:

Hello: Γεια σας (Yah sas)

Thank you: Ευχαριστώ (Efharistó)

Please: Παρακαλώ (Parakaló)

Yes: Ναι (Ne)

No: Όχι (Ohi)

Excuse me: Συγνώμη (Sygnómi)

Sorry: Λυπάμαι (Lypámai)

Goodbye: Αντίο (Adio)

Do you speak English?: Μιλάτε αγγλικά; (Miláte angliká?)

I don't understand: Δεν καταλαβαίνω (Den katalavéno)

Help: Βοήθεια (Voítheia)

How much is it?: Πόσο κοστίζει; (Póso kostízei?)

Where is...?: Πού είναι...; (Pú íne...?)

Can you recommend a good restaurant?: Μπορείτε να προτείνετε ένα καλό εστιατόριο; (Boríte na protínete éna kaló estiatório?)

Cheers!: Υγεία (Yiá sas)

Learning and using a few basic Greek phrases can go a long way in showing respect to the local culture and making meaningful connections with the people you meet during your travels in Kefalonia. Most locals will appreciate your efforts to communicate in their language, even if you only know a few words.

Emergency Contacts and Services

It's important to be aware of the emergency contacts and services available in Kefalonia. Here are some important numbers and information you should keep handy:

General Emergency Number: 112

The number 112 can be dialed for all emergency situations, including medical emergencies, accidents, and reporting crimes. This number is accessible from any phone, including mobile phones, and it connects you to the appropriate emergency service.

Medical Emergencies:

Ambulance: Dial 166

Kefalonia General Hospital (Argostoli): +30 26710 24641

Police:

Kefalonia Police: Dial 100

Argostoli Police Station: +30 26710 22222

Fire Department:

Fire Department: Dial 199

Tourist Police:

Tourist Police (Argostoli): +30 26710 22817

Pharmacy (Farmakeio):

Pharmacies can be found throughout Kefalonia. Look for the sign "Φαρμακείο" (Farmakeio) to locate one in your area. In case of an after-hours emergency, there is usually a rotating schedule for pharmacies to provide services outside regular hours.

Embassies and Consulates

It's advisable to have the contact information for your country's embassy or consulate in Greece in case you need assistance. Check the website of your embassy or consulate for their contact details.

It's also recommended to have travel insurance that covers medical emergencies and other unforeseen circumstances. Familiarize yourself with the details of your insurance coverage and keep a copy of your policy information easily accessible.

In case of any emergency, remain calm and provide clear information about the situation. If language is a barrier, the operators on the emergency line will try their best to assist you or may connect you with an interpreter.

Remember to always prioritize your safety and well-being.

It's a good practice to save the important emergency contact numbers in your phone or write them down in an easily accessible location during your trip to Kefalonia.

Antisamos Beach

CHAPTER 11

TIPS FOR RESPONSIBLE TRAVEL

Sustainable Tourism Practices

Choose eco-friendly accommodations that prioritize sustainability and minimize their environmental impact. Look for hotels or resorts with green certifications or those that implement energy-saving measures and waste reduction practices.

Conserve water and energy during your stay by practicing simple habits such as turning off lights and air conditioning when not in use, taking shorter showers, and reusing towels and linens.

Opt for public transportation or shared modes of transportation whenever possible to reduce carbon emissions. Explore Kefalonia by using buses, bicycles, or walking to experience the destination in a more sustainable way.

Supporting Local Communities

Engage with local businesses, such as restaurants, shops, and markets, to support the local economy. Choose authentic and locally-owned establishments to contribute to the livelihood of the local community.

Seek out local experiences, tours, and guides that provide an authentic perspective of Kefalonia's culture, traditions, and history. This supports local artisans, craftsmen, and small businesses while promoting cultural exchange.

Respect local customs, traditions, and social norms. Learn a few basic phrases in Greek to communicate with locals, show appreciation for their culture, and foster positive interactions.

Protecting the Environment

Follow designated trails and paths when exploring natural areas to avoid damaging fragile ecosystems. Be mindful of flora and fauna, and do not disturb or remove any plants or animals.

Properly dispose of waste by using designated recycling bins and waste management facilities. Avoid littering and consider carrying a reusable water bottle and shopping bag to minimize plastic waste.

When visiting beaches, avoid leaving any trash behind, including cigarette butts and plastic items. Help keep the beaches clean and preserve their natural beauty for future visitors to enjoy.

Local Customs and Etiquette

When visiting Kefalonia, it's important to be aware of the local customs and etiquette to show respect for the local culture. Here are some tips to help you navigate social interactions and embrace the customs of Kefalonia:

Greetings: Greeks often greet each other with a warm handshake and direct eye contact. When meeting someone for the first time or in more formal situations, it's polite to use their title (Mr., Mrs., or Miss) followed by their last name. Once a relationship is established, it's common to greet friends and acquaintances with a friendly kiss on each cheek.

Punctuality: While it's considered polite to arrive on time for scheduled appointments or meetings, Greeks tend to have a more relaxed attitude towards punctuality. If invited to someone's home, it's acceptable to arrive a little later than the specified time, usually within 15 minutes of the agreed-upon hour.

Respect for Elders: Greeks value respect for elders and hold them in high regard. It's customary to greet older individuals with deference and show respect for their wisdom and life experience.

Dining Etiquette: When invited to someone's home for a meal, it's customary to bring a small gift, such as a bottle of wine or dessert, as a token of appreciation. Greeks often enjoy long and leisurely meals, so be prepared for multiple courses and lively conversations. It's polite to wait for the host or hostess to initiate the start of the meal and to compliment the food throughout the dining experience.

Dress Code: While Kefalonia has a relaxed and casual atmosphere, it's respectful to dress modestly when visiting churches, monasteries, or other religious sites. It's advisable to avoid wearing revealing clothing or beach attire in such places. In general, Greeks appreciate a neat and tidy appearance.

Polite Gestures: Greeks use hand gestures during conversations to emphasize their points. It's common to use an open palm with fingers extended to indicate "stop" or "enough." The "OK" sign, formed by making a circle with your thumb and index finger, carries a different meaning in Greece and is considered vulgar. Be mindful of your gestures to avoid any unintentional offense.

Tipping: Tipping is appreciated but not obligatory in Kefalonia. It's customary to leave a tip of around 5-10% of the total bill in restaurants, cafes, or for other services, if you received good service. In some cases, a service charge may already be included, so check the bill before leaving an additional tip.

Remember, showing respect and understanding towards the local customs and traditions will enhance your interactions with the locals and create a more positive cultural exchange.

Recommended Reading and Resources

Here are some recommended reading materials and resources to enhance your knowledge and understanding of Kefalonia:

"Captain Corelli's Mandolin" by Louis de Bernières: This renowned novel is set on the island of Kefalonia during World War II and offers a captivating portrayal of the island's history and culture.

Visit Kefalonia and Visit Greece websites: These official tourism websites provide valuable information on attractions, events, accommodations, and practical tips for planning your trip to Kefalonia.

CONCLUSION

Kefalonia is a hidden gem waiting to be explored by travelers seeking natural beauty, rich history, and a tranquil escape. With its breathtaking beaches, picturesque villages, and diverse landscapes, this Greek island offers a unique blend of relaxation and adventure.

Whether you're diving into the crystal-clear waters of Myrtos Beach, exploring the enchanting Melissani Cave, or indulging in the local cuisine at traditional tavernas, Kefalonia promises an unforgettable experience. Immerse yourself in the island's fascinating history, marvel at its stunning vistas, and embrace the warm hospitality of the locals.

A trip to Kefalonia is sure to leave you with cherished memories and a longing to return to this paradise on earth.

TRAVEL PLANNERS

TRAVEL

DATE:

DURATION:

DESTINATION:

PLACES TO SEE:	LOCAL FOOD TO TRY:
1 _____	1 _____
2 _____	2 _____
3 _____	3 _____
4 _____	4 _____
5 _____	5 _____
6 _____	6 _____
7 _____	7 _____

DAY 1	DAY 2	DAY 3

DAY 4	DAY 5	DAY 6

NOTES	EXPENSES IN TOTAL:

PLANNER

TRAVEL

DATE:

DURATION:

DESTINATION:

PLACES TO SEE:	LOCAL FOOD TO TRY:
1	1
2	2
3	3
4	4
5	5
6	6
7	7

DAY 1	DAY 2	DAY 3

DAY 4	DAY 5	DAY 6

NOTES	EXPENSES IN TOTAL:

PLANNER

TRAVEL

DATE:

DURATION:

DESTINATION:

PLACES TO SEE:	LOCAL FOOD TO TRY:
1	1
2	2
3	3
4	4
5	5
6	6
7	7

DAY 1	DAY 2	DAY 3

DAY 4	DAY 5	DAY 6

NOTES	EXPENSES IN TOTAL:

PLANNER

TRAVEL

DATE:

DURATION:

DESTINATION:

PLACES TO SEE:	LOCAL FOOD TO TRY:
1	1
2	2
3	3
4	4
5	5
6	6
7	7

DAY 1	DAY 2	DAY 3

DAY 4	DAY 5	DAY 6

NOTES	EXPENSES IN TOTAL:

PLANNER

TRAVEL

DATE:

DURATION:

DESTINATION:

PLACES TO SEE:	LOCAL FOOD TO TRY:
1 _____	1 _____
2 _____	2 _____
3 _____	3 _____
4 _____	4 _____
5 _____	5 _____
6 _____	6 _____
7 _____	7 _____

DAY 1	DAY 2	DAY 3

DAY 4	DAY 5	DAY 6

NOTES	EXPENSES IN TOTAL:

PLANNER

TRAVEL

DATE:

DURATION:

DESTINATION:

PLACES TO SEE:	LOCAL FOOD TO TRY:
1 _____	1 _____
2 _____	2 _____
3 _____	3 _____
4 _____	4 _____
5 _____	5 _____
6 _____	6 _____
7 _____	7 _____

DAY 1	DAY 2	DAY 3

DAY 4	DAY 5	DAY 6

NOTES	EXPENSES IN TOTAL:

PLANNER

Printed in Great Britain
by Amazon